LEON

Fast Suppers

NATURALLY FAST RECIPES

LEON

Fast Suppers

NATURALLY FAST RECIPES

By Henry Dimbleby, Kay Plunkett-Hogge & John Vincent

PHOTOGRAPHY BY GEORGIA GLYNN SMITH · DESIGN BY ANITA MANGAN

conran
OCTOPUS

Contents

Introduction

We started Leon to make it easy for everyone to eat well. We'd begin, we decided, by creating what we coined 'Naturally Fast Food'. This book is that idea brought to life in 64 pages – a bottling of the elixir; all the power and mass of the naturally fast food universe condensed as if a few moments before the big bang.

We think this book is ideal for anyone who eats: anyone who eats well and wants to carry on that way, and anyone who eats badly but wants to eat well. We were in this second group in our twenties and that is why we began this mission. We were working too hard, and eating fast food or cold sandwiches for lunch that were making us fall asleep and wake up fat. With a spot. And when we got home, we would be too tired to work out what to cook, even though Henry is a trained chef and John was a (armchair) fan of good nutrition. These recipes for quick-to-make dishes that taste good and do you good helped us put an end to that. They'll also make you look cool. And attractive.

For a post-yoga (or maybe post-pub) cleanse, try the two broccoli dishes in our 'broccoli-off'. Natasha's Chicken Fajitas are a joy for children – as they would say at Chessington World of Adventures – 'of all ages'. Easy Pad Thai is a gift to the world from our friend Kay Plunkett-Hogge and a gift for you to share with friends. The Keralan Fish Curry is a healthy and cost-effective way of experiencing the south of India without the jet lag. Finally, like all the recipes in this book, cooking, sharing and eating the Ceviche will make you very happy. It will take you to a better place. Like…the garden.

Enough introduction – we hope you love cooking these dishes and that they set you up for brilliant evenings and energetic mornings-after.

Happy cooking.

Henry & John

SIMPLICITY ITSELF

Carpaccio with Parmesan Crisp

Very quick, much easier than people think, and super-impressive.

½ teaspoon **coriander seeds**
½ teaspoon **cumin seeds**
½ teaspoon **sea salt**
½ teaspoon **freshly ground black pepper**
500g **fillet** or **sirloin steak** (a tender good-quality one)
2 tablespoons **extra virgin olive oil**
a lime-sized lump of **Parmesan cheese**
1 tablespoon **crème fraîche** or **fromage frais**
a handful of **rocket leaves**
1 tablespoon **balsamic vinegar**

1. Grind the spices, salt and pepper together and rub well into the steak. Sear the outside of the meat in a hot pan for 1 minute with 1 tablespoon of the olive oil. Remove it from the pan, let it cool then wrap it in clingfilm and put into the fridge.

2. Grate the Parmesan super-fine and sprinkle it in an even layer on to a hot non-stick pan. It will bubble and go slightly golden. Slide it off with a spatula and leave on a piece of kitchen paper. As it cools, it will crisp up.

3. Slice the meat finely and arrange it on a plate with blobs of crème fraîche. Sprinkle the rocket on top, and drizzle with the balsamic vinegar and the remaining olive oil. Season. Break the Parmesan crisp into pieces and scatter on top.

TIPS

* You can place the steak under clingfilm after searing and slicing, and whack it with a rolling pin if you want it super-fine. We never bother, but you can if you want to.

* For variations on this theme, see page 13.

Justin Ovenden's Mackerel Ceviche

SERVES 4 • PREPARATION TIME: 15 MINUTES • COOKING TIME: NONE • ♥ ✓ WF GF DF

First things first: ceviche is not raw fish (that's sushi). You're cooking it chemically in the acid from the lime juice. Even so, you want really fresh mackerel for this, the fresher the better.

Justin says: 'This is very much a "what's in the garden, how's it looking" dish, so don't worry if you go a little over or under on the measurements.'

> 4 large **mackerel fillets**, skinned and boned
> the juice of 1 (or 2) **limes**
> 1 tablespoon **olive oil** or **rapeseed oil**
> 1–3 small **red chillies**, finely chopped, depending on heat tolerance
> a small handful of **fresh chives**, finely chopped
> a handful of **rocket leaves**
> a small handful of **fresh coriander** and/or **hyssop**
> a small bunch of **baby asparagus**, lightly steamed
> **rock salt** and **coarse ground black pepper**

1. Cut the mackerel into roughly 1cm squares or strips. Mix it with the lime juice, oil, chillies and chives, and season with salt and pepper.

2. Leave to stand for 5–10 minutes, giving it an occasional stir. Then mix it with the leaves, herbs and asparagus and serve.

TIPS

* Hyssop is a very ancient herb with a slightly bitter, minty flavour. Be careful when you're cooking with it – like sage, it has a tendency to dominate.

JUSTIN, 1975

Six Ways with Ceviche

A great ceviche requires a sharp marinated fishy element and a sweet element. You can use the same technique to make any number of variations. These are some that we have tried in the past. Keep the onion, chilli, oil and coriander from the recipe on page 15 and replace the fish, radish and avocado with the listed ingredients.

English:
Finely sliced scallops and pea shoots.

Scottish:
Wild salmon and very finely sliced fennel.

West Indian:
Finely sliced large, raw prawns with mango and avocado.

Vegetarian:
Courgettes, sliced thinly into tongues using a peeler.

Peruvian:
Sea bass with small chunks of roasted sweet potato.

and an added bonus…
Leche de tigre (tiger's milk): Mix the liquid that runs off the ceviche with ice-cold vodka. A great aperitif or hangover cure.

Six Ways with Carpaccio

Once you have your basic carpaccio recipe (see page 10) down pat, you can play with all sorts of variations for the toppers. Our favourites include:

Classic:
Drizzled with a mustardy dressing.

Continental:
Capers, olive oil and baby spinach leaves.

British:
Little roast beetroots with horseradish cream and watercress.

Summer:
Finely shaved fennel in a light lemon and olive oil dressing.

Fusion:
Finely sliced chillies and a drizzle of soy sauce.

Posh:
Parmesan shavings, olive oil and finely sliced black truffle.

Sea Bass Ceviche

SERVES 4 (AS A STARTER OR LIGHT LUNCH) • PREPARATION TIME: 15 MINUTES •
COOKING TIME: NONE • ♥ ✓ WF GF DF

A simple, stunning and super-fresh dish for a hot summer's day. The lemon juice 'cooks' the fish delicately. Eat with a glass of white wine so cold there's a kind of mist on the side of the glass.

½ a **fresh red chilli**
½ a **red onion**
a handful of **radishes** (the
    bigger each radish the better)
250g **sea bass fillet**
    (equivalent to a 600g bass),
    boned and skinned

juice of 1 **lemon**
3 tablespoons **extra virgin olive
    oil**, plus extra for drizzling
1 **avocado**
a small bunch of **fresh coriander**
sea salt and **freshly ground
    black pepper**

1. Deseed and slice the chilli into fine strips and peel and slice the red onion as fine as you can manage. Slice the radishes very thinly.

2. Finely slice the sea bass into strips and put it in a bowl with the chilli, onion and radishes together with the lemon juice and olive oil.

3. Season well with salt and pepper – this is very important with ceviche.

4. You have a very simple balance of flavours, so take time to get the seasoning just right. Add more chilli and lemon juice if necessary.

5. Leave for 10 minutes – and no more (less if you like it a little sushi-style). If you leave it for too long the fish will 'overcook'.

6. Peel the avocado and cut in half, remove the stone and slice each half into delicate half moons. Arrange the fish mixture on a large plate, pour over any remaining lemon marinade and drizzle with a little extra olive oil. Scatter over the coriander leaves and serve.

TIPS

* In Peru this is a national dish. They often eat it as a simple lunch – *almuerzo* – with baked sweet potato. The orange colour and sweet taste of the potato make a wonderful switch for the avocado in this recipe.

* Ceviche is one of those dishes you can experiment with. Try lime juice instead of lemon. Change the fish – use scallops, raw prawns or salmon. Use pieces of grilled corn on the cob from the barbecue instead of avocado. See more ideas on page 13.

Salmon in a Bag Three Ways

SERVES 4 • PREPARATION TIME: 10–15 MINUTES • COOKING TIME: 15–20 MINUTES

Even people who say they don't really like fish seem to like salmon. Pink and juicy, it's packed with all sorts of good-for-you goodies. It's high in protein, in vitamins D and B12, and don't forget those omega-3 fatty acids – good for the heart, limbs and the old brain. Top food.

This method of cooking salmon (en papillote) is super-quick and easy. Essentially, you're steaming the fish in a 'bag' so you lose none of its goodness. Here are three of our favourites.

1. Heat the oven to 180°C/350°F/gas mark 4.

2. Pop each salmon fillet on to a square of either greaseproof paper or foil measuring about 35 x 35cm. Then add the flavourings and the liquids, depending on which version you're making. Seal the 'bag' or parcel with tight folds, making sure there's room inside for the salmon to steam. If you're using greaseproof paper, don't scrunch instead of folding as this may unravel, spilling all those precious salmon juices.

3. Place the parcels on a baking tray and cook them in the oven for 15 minutes, or until the salmon is just cooked through.

4. Remove from the oven and place carefully on to plates. Then rush them to the table so that everyone can open their own bag and add their own garnish.

Provençal Salmon ♥ ✓ WF GF DF

These flavours always remind us of summers in France.

4 **salmon fillets**, about 140g each
8 **cherry tomatoes**, or 4 larger
   tomatoes, halved
16 **black olives**
2 cloves of **garlic**, peeled
   and chopped

a handful of **fresh basil leaves**,
   plus a little extra to garnish
a drizzle of **olive oil**
a splash of **dry white vermouth**
salt and **freshly ground
   black pepper**

St Clement's Salmon ♥ ✓ WF GF DF

Oranges and lemons, say the bells of St. Clement's…

4 **salmon fillets**, about 140g each
4 thin slices of **lemon**
4 thin slices of **orange**
2–3 sprigs of **fresh dill**, finely
   chopped
2 cloves of **garlic**, peeled and
   chopped
juice of ½ a **lemon**

juice of ½ an **orange** (you should
   have about 4 tablespoons of
   liquid from the two halved
   fruits)
a drizzle of **olive oil**
a few sprigs of **fresh dill**, to garnish
salt and **freshly ground
   black pepper**

Thai Salmon ♥ ✓ WF GF DF

Exotic and warming, with some fiery red chilli…

4 **salmon fillets**, about 140g each
1 **red bird's-eye chilli**, deseeded
   and finely chopped
2 **coriander roots**, chopped
2 cloves of **garlic**, chopped
1 tablespoon **nam pla** (fish sauce)

2 **spring onions**, trimmed and
   chopped
2 tablespoons **lime juice**
a good grinding of **white pepper**
a bunch of **fresh coriander**,
   to garnish

Perfect Pepper Steak

SERVES 2 • PREPARATION TIME: 10 MINUTES PLUS MACERATING • COOKING TIME: 10–15 MINUTES • WF

Pepper steak, or steak au poivre, is a bistro classic that we all take for granted. And it's one which, because it's so simple, is all too often made really badly. We think this recipe gets it just about right, all the way down to the retro 70s whisky cream sauce.

2 **steaks** of your choice
1 clove of **garlic**, halved
1 teaspoon **olive oil**
1 tablespoon **whole white peppercorns**, coarsely crushed
1 tablespoon **whole black peppercorns**, coarsely crushed
1 tablespoon **coarse sea salt**
100ml **whisky** (optional)
125ml **double cream** (optional)
1 tablespoon **green peppercorns**, rinsed (optional)

1. Pat the steaks dry and rub the cut side of the garlic liberally over both sides of each steak, then rub with the olive oil.

2. Pat the pepper on to the steaks and leave to macerate for an hour. (If you're in a hurry, don't worry – the steaks just won't be as peppery.)

3. Heat a wide frying pan as hot as you dare. Season the steaks with the sea salt then slap the meat in the pan. Now, here's the thing – every steak has its own time scale. We swear by the following test: Hold out your left hand. With your right hand, feel that fleshy bit of palm under your thumb. You'll see it goes from soft and squishy to hard by

A SHORT PHOTO STORY ...

READY TO PLAY 70s COP SHOW

KEEP YOUR EYE ON THE TARGET

THE CHASE HAS BEGUN

your wrist. Keep touching the steaks with your finger. Soft and squishy = rare: medium = medium; hard = well done. It really is the best way.

4. When the steaks are cooked just how you like them, set them aside on a warm plate to rest for at least 5 minutes. This is very important. It lets the fibres of the meat relax and the flavours develop.

5. While the steaks are resting, if liked, deglaze the pan with the whisky, then pour in the cream. Bubble it up so the cream thickens for about a minute, then add the green peppercorns. Pour the sauce over the steaks, and serve with a green salad, or a baked potato and spinach.

COVER ME

QUICK SNACK

AND A SIT DOWN, TIME FOR TEA

BURGERS, WRAPS & FAJITAS

Fred's Classic Beef Burger

SERVES 4 • PREPARATION TIME: 10 MINUTES • COOKING TIME: 10–15 MINUTES • ✓ WF GF

This is about as simple as it gets: just beef, onion, salt and pepper. Fred says he used to mess around with it a lot more, but he made so many burgers for his chums during Euro 96, and this was the version everyone preferred.

1 **onion**, peeled and cut into chunks
450g good-quality **minced beef**
1 tablespoon **olive oil** or **vegetable oil**
salt and **freshly ground black pepper**

1. In a food processor, blitz the onion into tiny pieces. Add the minced beef and pulse just enough to mix the onion into it. You don't want to be too over-zealous here, or you'll end up with a meat paste. We want it well blended, but with texture.

2. Turn the meat mixture out into a bowl and season well with salt and pepper, mixing it together thoroughly with your hands. Now divide it into 4 equal-sized patties.

3. Heat a non-stick frying pan over a medium–high heat. Rub both sides of the patties with olive oil and season them again with salt and pepper. Then pop them into the pan. Fry for 10–15 minutes, turning once or twice, until they're cooked how you like them. Serve in a bun, with lettuce, cheese, ketchup and mustard.

'Ciao Bella' Italian Burger

SERVES 4 • PREPARATION TIME: 10 MINUTES • COOKING TIME: 10–15 MINUTES • ✓

Think Sophia Loren in a bun.

1 **onion**, peeled and cut into chunks
1 clove of **garlic**, peeled
1 sprig of **fresh rosemary**, leaves picked
3 sprigs of **fresh flat-leaf parsley**, leaves picked
170g **minced veal**
170g **minced pork**
170g **minced beef**
1 tablespoon **olive oil**
salt and **freshly ground black pepper**

1. In a food processor, blitz the onion, garlic and herb leaves. Add the meat and pulse to blend it together.

2. Turn the mixture out into a bowl and season with salt and pepper, working the seasonings in thoroughly with your hands. Now divide it into 4 equal-sized patties.

3. Heat a non-stick frying pan over a medium–high heat. Rub the patties on both sides with the olive oil and season with salt and pepper. Fry them for 15–20 minutes, turning once or twice, or until they're cooked to your liking.

4. Serve in ciabatta rolls, with lettuce, tomato and maybe some mostarda di frutta or a spiky onion relish.

The Veggie Burger

SERVES 4 • PREPARATION TIME: 10 MINUTES • COOKING TIME: 15 MINUTES • ✓

This is not your usual veggie burger bulked up with beans, this is just veggies pure and simple.

2 tablespoons **olive oil** (more if you are cooking in 2 batches)
4 large **Portabello mushrooms**, about 150g each, trimmed and wiped
1 **red pepper**, deseeded and cut into 8 rings
3–4 cloves of **garlic**, peeled and chopped
a good handful of **fresh parsley**, chopped
1 **avocado**, peeled, stoned and sliced
4 **wholemeal rolls** (or rolls of your choice), to serve
salt and **freshly ground black pepper**

1. Heat 1 tablespoon of the olive oil in a wide frying pan. Pop in the mushrooms and gently fry them, turning occasionally until they are just done – about 5–7 minutes in all. Remove the mushrooms from the pan with a slotted spoon and set aside.

2. Heat the remaining tablespoon of olive oil. Sauté the red pepper rings until they start to colour, but are still crisp. Remove them from the pan and set aside. Pop in the garlic and parsley and sauté until softened and fragrant – just a couple of minutes.

3. Reintroduce the mushrooms to the pan, along with any juices that have come from them. Stir to mix everything thoroughly and season with salt and pepper.

4. Place the mushrooms on the halved rolls. Pop two red pepper rings on top of each, a few slices of avocado and top with mayo.

Spicy Thai Pork Burger

SERVES 4 • PREPARATION TIME: 10 MINUTES • COOKING TIME: 15–20 MINUTES • ✓

We saw something similar to this served rather innovatively between two discs of sticky rice in northern Thailand. So we decided to create our own.

1½ tablespoons **white peppercorns**
2cm **fresh ginger**, peeled and chopped
3 **coriander roots**
3 cloves of **garlic**, peeled
a pinch of **salt**
500g **minced pork**
1 tablespoon **nam pla** (fish sauce)
1 tablespoon chopped **fresh coriander**
2 tablespoons **vegetable oil**

1. Grind the peppercorns in a pestle and mortar. Then add the chopped ginger, coriander roots, garlic and a pinch of salt, and grind them into the pepper until you have a dry paste.

2. Put the paste into a bowl, add the minced pork, along with the nam pla and the fresh coriander, and work all the ingredients together. (You can do this in a food processor, just don't blitz it too hard.) Form into 4 even-sized patties.

3. Heat the oil in a non-stick frying pan and fry the patties for about 15–20 minutes, turning them from time to time until they're cooked through. Serve in a soft white bap, with mayonnaise, sriracha sauce, crisp lettuce and a slice of cucumber or tomato.

TIPS

* White pepper is a key ingredient in Thai food. By all means, cut down the pepperiness if you like, but leave in at least half a tablespoonful or the burger will be very bland.

Kay's California Rock 'n' Roll Wrap

This is loosely based on the idea of the California roll you get in Japanese restaurants.

300g **salmon fillet**
2 tablespoons **light soy sauce** or **tamari**
4 tablespoons good **mayonnaise**
½ teaspoon **wasabi powder** (more if you like it hot)
4 **wraps** of your choice, warmed
3 **spring onions**, trimmed and shredded lengthways
1 **avocado**, peeled, stoned and sliced
1–2 tablespoons **toasted sesame seeds**
1 **lime**, quartered (optional)

1. Heat the oven to 200°C/400°F/gas mark 6 or preheat the grill.

2. Marinate the salmon in the soy sauce for a few minutes. Then either grill or bake it in the oven for about 12–15 minutes depending on its thickness, or until it's cooked (you can follow the recipe for Sweet Soy Salmon on page 46 if you like).

3. Mix the mayonnaise with the wasabi powder.

4. Put the salmon into the wrap with some shredded spring onion, sliced avocado, wasabi mayonnaise and a sprinkling of toasted sesame seeds. Serve with a wedge of lime, if liked.

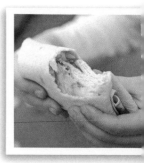

Natasha's Chicken Fajitas

SERVES 4 • PREPARATION TIME: 10 MINUTES PLUS MARINATING • COOKING TIME: 15 MINUTES • ♥ DF

John's daughter Natasha's favourite dinner is fajitas. Saturday night, Sunday night, any night. In front of *Glee*: eleven-year-old girl heaven.

> 3 small boneless and skinless **chicken breasts**, cut into strips
> 2 teaspoons **dried oregano**
> a good pinch of **chilli powder**, or to taste
> 1 teaspoon **ground cumin**
> 1 **onion**, peeled and thinly sliced
> 2 **red peppers**, thinly sliced
> 3 tablespoons **olive oil**
> 4 **flatbreads** of your choice, or some soft **tortilla**
> **salt** and **freshly ground black pepper**

1. Put the chicken, oregano, chilli, cumin, onion and peppers into a bowl with 2 tablespoons of the olive oil and mix well. Season with salt and pepper and set aside to marinate for as long as you can.

2. Heat the remaining tablespoon of olive oil in a sauté pan over a medium heat and add the chicken, onion and peppers. Cook until the onions have caught some colour, the peppers are soft and the chicken is cooked through – about 7–10 minutes. You may need to do this in 2 batches to make sure the chicken browns up nicely.

3. Serve in a flatbread or tortilla with lettuce, if liked, and with a bowl of pepper and chilli salsa or guacamole on the side.

PASTA

Linguine with Crab & Tomato

SERVES 4 • PREPARATION TIME: 10 MINUTES • COOKING TIME: 10–12 MINUTES • DF

This is Kay's absolute favourite pasta sauce.

400g **linguine**
3 tablespoons **olive oil**
2 cloves of **garlic**, peeled and
    finely chopped
1 **red serrano** or other **medium-hot
    chilli**, deseeded and sliced
    into small pieces
8–12 **cherry tomatoes**
250g **white crabmeat** or
    2 x 170g tins of **crab**

2 tablespoons **dry white
    vermouth** or **white wine**
2 tablespoons **dark crabmeat**
1 tablespoon chopped **fresh
    flat-leaf parsley**
salt and **freshly ground
    black pepper**

1. Bring a large pan of salted water up to a rolling boil. Check the cooking time on your pasta pack – we find, normally, for al dente pasta, that it takes a little less time than advertised – and pop in the linguine.

2. Meanwhile, heat 2 tablespoons of olive oil in a large sauté pan over a medium heat. Add the garlic and stir until you can just smell it. Now add the chilli and the tomatoes. Stir until the garlic just begins to colour, then add the white crabmeat or tinned crab. Stir for a moment or two, then add the vermouth or wine, the dark crabmeat and a good pinch of the parsley. Season with salt and pepper and stir together well. All in, this should take no more than 5 minutes.

3. If the pasta isn't quite cooked, set the sauce aside to keep warm. When the linguine's done, drain it and toss in the remaining tablespoon of olive oil. Stir the crabmeat sauce through the pasta and serve with a sprinkling of parsley and a good grind of black pepper. Oh, and with a good glass of crisp Italian white.

TIPS

* We often make this with tinned crab and without the dark crabmeat – it's a quick and easy storecupboard staple. But if you really want to go for it, buy ready-prepared crabmeat – we like the white and dark crabmeat pots from Seafood and Eat It.

* The wine or vermouth adds a dimension to this dish, but you can substitute water.

Tom's Red Pesto Surprise

SERVES 4 • PREPARATION TIME: 5 MINUTES • COOKING TIME: 20 MINUTES • DF

Ideal comfort food, and perfect for curing a lingering hangover. No one has quite worked out what the surprise is yet.

5 cloves of **garlic**
2 **onions**
250g **smoked streaky bacon**
3 tablespoons **olive oil**
350g **frozen peas**
400g **penne**
3–4 tablespoons good **red pesto**
salt

1. Put a pan of salted water on to boil. Peel and finely chop the garlic and onions, and cut the bacon into small chunks.

2. Fry the garlic and onions in the olive oil in a large, heavy-based frying pan for 5 minutes. Add the chopped bacon and cook for a further 3 minutes. Add the peas and stir well, coating them well with oil, then cook for around 10 minutes on a slow heat.

3. While the sauce is simmering, cook your pasta according to the instructions on the packet, and drain, retaining 1 tablespoon of the cooking water. Put the pasta back into the pan with the reserved water to keep it moist.

4. When the peas are cooked and you are ready to eat, stir in the pesto. Add the pasta, and stir well. Serve immediately.

TIPS

* The key is not to be mean with your pesto. If you feel it needs more, add more.

TA-DA !

Pasta with Peas

SERVES 4 • PREPARATION TIME: 5 MINUTES • COOKING TIME: 15 MINUTES • ♥ V

Even in the depths of a nuclear winter, you could probably rustle together the ingredients for this dish – unsophisticated but cosy, perfect for a TV dinner.

2 **onions**
3 cloves of **garlic**
2 **leeks**
4 tablespoons **olive oil**
a thumb-sized blob of **butter**
400g **penne**
200g **frozen peas**
juice of 1 **lemon**
freshly grated Parmesan cheese, to taste
sea salt and **freshly ground black pepper**

1. Peel and roughly chop the onions and garlic. Then trim and slice the leeks thinly.

2. Heat the oil and butter in a pan over a medium heat. Add the onions and soften for a few minutes.

3. Add the leeks and garlic, stir, and leave over a very low heat with the lid on. Check and stir every so often to make sure the leeks aren't browning. You may need to add a few drops of water (or white wine if you have some to hand).

4. Meanwhile, put the pasta on to boil. Two minutes before it is due to be ready, stir the peas and lemon juice into the leek and onion mixture and continue to cook over a medium heat until the peas are just cooked through. Season to taste.

5. Drain the pasta, return it to the pan, stir in the vegetables and serve in bowls, topped with generous handfuls of Parmesan.

TOP: PASTA WITH PEAS
BOTTOM: SPAGHETTI PUTTANESCA

TIPS

* If you don't have any leeks, mushrooms are lovely. Sliced red peppers are not bad either.

Spaghetti Puttanesca

SERVES 4 • PREPARATION TIME: 5 MINUTES • COOKING TIME: 25 MINUTES • ♥ DF

Take all the greatest-tasting storecupboard ingredients, turn them into a spaghetti sauce and this is what you get (see picture on page 34).

2 cloves of **garlic**
1 x 50g tin of **anchovies**
1 tablespoon **capers**
4 tablespoons **extra virgin olive oil**
1 **dried chilli** or 1 teaspoon **chilli powder**
1 teaspoon **dried oregano**
150g (about 2 small) **white onions**
100g drained pitted **black olives**
1 x 400g tin of **chopped tomatoes**
400g **spaghetti**
freshly grated Parmesan cheese, to taste (optional)
sea salt and **freshly ground black pepper**

1. Fill a pan with salted water and bring it to the boil.

2. Peel and finely chop the garlic, and finely chop the anchovies and capers. Heat the oil in a frying pan over a medium heat, and add the chopped ingredients. Crumble in the dried chilli and oregano, and allow to brown gently.

3. Peel and finely chop the onions and add to the pan with the olives. Coat everything well and pour in the tomatoes together with 100ml of water. Increase the heat so that the sauce is bubbling. Stir regularly and cook until the tomatoes have become darker.

4. Cook your spaghetti as per the packet instructions, then drain but retain a few tablespoons of water to keep the pasta loose. Tip the pasta into the sauce and mix slowly and well, using 2 forks. Top with black pepper and Parmesan if you fancy, and serve.

TIPS

* Add a chopped fresh chilli for extra fire.
* Clearly this will go well with other pastas besides spaghetti.
* A little chopped parsley added at the end freshens it up nicely.

Tagliatelle Aglio, Olio e Peperoncino

SERVES 2 • PREPARATION TIME: 5 MINUTES • COOKING TIME: 10–12 MINUTES

This is one of the world's simplest dishes to make, and one of the most satisfying, too.

200g **tagliatelle**
2 tablespoons **olive oil**
1–2 cloves of **garlic**, peeled and sliced
1 teaspoon **dried chilli flakes** or 1 **fresh red chilli**, sliced
1 tablespoon finely chopped **fresh flat-leaf parsley** (optional)
freshly grated Parmesan cheese, to taste
salt and **freshly ground black pepper**

1. Bring a large pan of salted water to a rolling boil and cook the pasta according to the packet instructions.

2. Put the olive oil into a heavy-based sauté pan over a low–medium heat and add the garlic and the chilli. Cook until the garlic turns a deep golden brown.When the pasta's done, use a pair of tongs to scoop it into the garlic, chilli and oil.

3. You want a little residual cooking water to go with it. Stir everything together, season with salt, pepper and the parsley, if using, and serve at once with a good sprinkling of freshly grated Parmesan.

TIPS

* You can make this with most of the longer pastas, spaghetti, linguine, capellini… we wouldn't go for one that's much fatter than tagliatelle, and as for pasta shapes, well, there really isn't enough sauce here to get deliciously caught in their crenellations, so what's the point?

LEON IN PRAIA DA ROCHA, 1965

Things That Taste Good on Top of Pasta

Anchovies and cream
Melt the anchovies in a little oil until they break up then mix in the cream and plenty of pepper.

Butter, pepper and herbs
Chop the herbs finely and turn everything into the hot pasta.

Garlic breadcrumbs
Fry the breadcrumbs in some olive oil with finely chopped garlic, salt and pepper.

Blue cheese
Simply crumble over the hot pasta with a little butter and pepper.

Pecans, parsley, basil and chilli
Warm some olive oil gently in a pan. Chop everything finely, drop into the olive oil, stir briefly then turn into the pasta.

Almonds and garlic
Finely chop the garlic and melt gently in some butter. Turn through pasta. Season. Add the almonds on top.

HOT & SPICY

John's Broccoli

WITH GARLIC, CASHEW NUTS & CHILLI

SERVES 4 • PREPARATION TIME: 5 MINUTES • COOKING TIME: 10 MINUTES • ♥ ✓ WF GF DF V

The combination of chillies, soy sauce and cashews helps make this very healthy dish a triumph of flavour. Simple and speedy.

500g **broccoli**
3 cloves of **garlic**, peeled
2 **red chillies**
2 tablespoons **rapeseed oil** or **groundnut oil**
a small handful of **cashews**
a hearty splash of **light soy sauce**
1 **lime**, cut into quarters

1. Cut the broccoli into medium-sized florets and steam them lightly over boiling water so that they are partly cooked.

2. Peel and finely slice the garlic and chillies. Put them into a large frying pan over a medium heat with the rapeseed or groundnut oil and fry until starting to soften.

3. Add the cashews and broccoli and stir well, so that everything is coated with oil and golden garlic.

4. Add the soy sauce, cover with a lid and cook for a further 2 minutes.

5. Finish each serving with a squeeze of lime.

TIPS

* This can be turned into a more substantial dish for 4 people by adding 2 fillets of salmon.

Joanna's Purple Sprouting Broccoli

WITH SAUSAGE, CHILLI & FENNEL

SERVES 4 • PREPARATION TIME: 10 MINUTES • COOKING TIME: 20 MINUTES • ✓ WF DF

Our friend Joanna Weinburg taught us how to make this. Supper or lunch in just one bowl, with a surprising depth of flavour for such a simple dish.

4 cloves of **garlic**
1 tablespoon **extra virgin olive oil**
½ teaspoon **dried chilli flakes**
2 teaspoons **fennel seeds**
800g plain best-quality **pork sausage meat** (or **sausages**, squeezed out of their skins)
800g **purple sprouting broccoli**
juice of 1 **lemon**

1. Peel and roughly chop the garlic, then heat the oil in a frying pan and gently fry the chilli, garlic and fennel seeds until the garlic is golden.

2. Crumble in the sausage meat, turning it well in the mixture and breaking it up. Fry until the bottom becomes golden, then turn and break up again.

3. Chop the broccoli roughly and add to the pan. Turn well to coat it in the oil. Partly cover the dish and leave to cook for 5–7 minutes. The broccoli will still be crunchy.

4. Stir again, squeeze over the lemon juice, divide between plates and eat immediately.

* The key is to use a large pan so you have plenty of room to break up the sausage meat and brown it. If the pan is too crowded, it will steam instead.

TIPS

Easy Pad Thai

SERVES 2 • PREPARATION TIME: 10 MINUTES • COOKING TIME: 5–10 MINUTES • WF GF DF

This has nothing on the Pad Thai at Pratu Pee (the Ghost's Gate) in Bangkok, but it's pretty darn good, and streamlined for speed. It's better to make this in small batches, so the recipe here feeds 2. If you prefer, you can change the prawns for the same amount of chicken or pork.

150g **rice noodles**
1 tablespoon **vegetable oil**
3 cloves of **garlic**, peeled and chopped
150–200g **raw peeled prawns**
2 **free-range eggs**, lightly beaten
2 handfuls of **bean sprouts**
2 **spring onions**, trimmed and chopped
2 tablespoons **dried prawns**
2 tablespoons **unsalted, roasted peanuts**, roughly chopped
3 tablespoons **nam pla** (fish sauce)
2 tablespoons **lime juice**

2 tablespoons **granulated sugar**
¼ teaspoon **chilli powder**
½ teaspoon **tamarind purée**

For the garnish:
2 **spring onions**, trimmed and chopped
1 tablespoon **fresh coriander**, leaves picked
a few slices of **cucumber** (optional)
½ tablespoon roasted unsalted **peanuts**, roughly chopped
2 **lime** wedges

1. Soak the rice noodles in warm water for 5–10 minutes, or until they're just malleable. (The instructions on the packet will probably say to soak them for 15–20 minutes, but this will make them too soggy for the finished dish.) Drain, rinse and set aside.

2. Heat the oil in a wok over a high heat. Add the garlic and stir-fry quickly until just turning golden. Add the fresh prawns and stir-fry for a minute or two. Then add the noodles and stir through before adding the eggs, bean sprouts, spring onions, dried prawns and peanuts, stirring after each addition.

3. When everything is well combined, add the nam pla, lime juice, sugar, chilli powder and tamarind purée. Stir thoroughly, then serve at once, garnished with spring onions, coriander, cucumber and peanuts, with lime wedges on the side.

Sweet Soy Salmon

WITH MUSHROOMS & PEA SHOOTS

SERVES 4 • PREPARATION TIME: 15 MINUTES • COOKING TIME: 8–10 MINUTES • ✓ DF

A Japanese-inflected salmon. The wasabi provides a punch that salmon takes really well. For an extra kick try adding a pinch of dried chilli flakes.

4 **salmon steaks**, about
125–150g each
4 tablespoons **tamari**
1–2 teaspoons **wasabi paste**,
or to taste
2 teaspoons **granulated sugar**
4 teaspoons **rice vinegar**
1 tablespoon **olive oil**, plus
1 teaspoon
a 2cm piece of **fresh ginger**,
peeled and finely slivered
4 **spring onions**, trimmed and
sliced on the diagonal

3 cloves of **garlic**, peeled
and chopped
100g **fresh shiitake** and/
or **girolles mushrooms**,
trimmed and sliced
a pinch of **dried chilli**
(optional)
a squeeze of **lemon juice**
50g **pea shoots**
salt and **freshly ground
black pepper**

1. Heat the oven to 200°C/400°F/gas mark 6.

2. Put the salmon into a small roasting tray. Mix the tamari, wasabi, sugar, vinegar and the teaspoon of oil together in a bowl, and pour over the fish, coating it well.

3. Divide up the slivers of ginger and half the sliced spring onions into 4 little piles, and sprinkle one evenly over each piece of salmon. Season with a pinch of pepper, and roast for about 8 minutes, or until the salmon is just cooked through.

4. While the salmon is in the oven, heat the tablespoon of olive oil in a frying pan over a medium heat. When it's hot, add the garlic and cook until soft but not browned. Now add the mushrooms and cook for a few minutes, making sure that all the water evaporates out of them, otherwise they'll be soggy (mushrooms are 90% water). Add the pinch of chilli, if you like, a squeeze of lemon juice and the rest

of the spring onions and continue cooking for a few minutes. Remove from the heat, and season with a little salt and pepper.

5. Remove the salmon from the oven and pop it on to 4 plates. Top with the mushroom mixture and finish with an even scattering of the pea shoots.

TIPS

* When pea shoots are out of season, use watercress or rocket leaves.

* You could also mix in 100g of frozen peas or some edamame beans when cooking the mushrooms.

* Experiment with different mushrooms – chestnut mushrooms work just as well, as do enoki.

Keralan Fish Curry

SERVES 4 • PREPARATION TIME: 10 MINUTES • COOKING TIME: 20 MINUTES • ✓ WF GF DF

This is a simple south Indian fish curry.

1 **green chilli**
1 teaspoon **rapeseed oil**,
    to make the paste
1 teaspoon **ground coriander**
½ teaspoon **turmeric**
5 cloves of **garlic**, peeled
2.5cm piece of **fresh ginger**, peeled
1 tablespoon **coconut oil**
    or **rapeseed oil**

½ teaspoon **fenugreek seeds**
4 small **onions**
100ml **coconut milk**
400g **mackerel fillets**, cut into
    5cm pieces
sea salt and **freshly ground
    black pepper**

1. Deseed the chilli and put it into a blender with the rapeseed oil, coriander, turmeric, and peeled garlic and ginger and whizz to form a paste.

2. Heat the coconut oil in a pan and sauté the paste and the fenugreek seeds.

3. Peel the onions, slice finely and add them to the pan with the coconut milk and 300ml of water. Season really well with salt and pepper. Bring to the boil and keep it at a gentle boil until the sauce reduces, which should take about 5 minutes.

4. Cut the mackerel into 5cm pieces and add to the curry. Simmer gently until the fish is cooked through, which should take somewhere between 5 and 8 minutes.

TIPS

* Best served with rice.
* You can use prawns or white fish if mackerel is too strong for your taste.
* The mackerel should be very fresh, as it develops too strong a flavour if kept for too long in the fridge.

TOP: HONEYMOON VEGETABLE CURRY
BOTTOM: KERALAN FISH CURRY

Honeymoon Vegetable Curry

SERVES 4 • PREPARATION TIME: 15 MINUTES • COOKING TIME: 20 MINUTES • ✓ WF GF DF V

Not the most beautiful of curries, but a great staple for a simple healthy supper
(pictured on page 49).

> 4 **courgettes**
> 2 **carrots**
> 2 **aubergines**
> ¼ of an **onion**
> 2 **green chillies**
> 200ml **coconut milk**
> ½ teaspoon **ground cumin**
> ¼ teaspoon **turmeric**
> 1 **lime**
> **sea salt** and **freshly ground black pepper**

1. Chop the courgettes into diagonal slices. Peel and chop the carrots
   into chunky batons and chop the aubergines into cubes. Peel and
   chop the onion roughly, and deseed the chillies.

2. Place the coconut milk, chillies, onion and cumin into a food
   processor and whizz to a paste.

3. Dry fry the turmeric in a pan for a minute, then add the vegetables
   and 200ml of water. Bring to the boil, then reduce the heat and
   simmer for about 15 minutes, or until tender.

4. Add the coconut milk paste and cook gently for another 5 minutes.

5. Season, and squeeze over the juice of the lime before serving.

TIPS

* Serve on white basmati rice.

Kay's Pad Krapow Neua

(STIR-FRIED BEEF WITH HOLY BASIL)

SERVES 2 AS A MAIN COURSE OR 4 AS PART OF A LARGER THAI MEAL •
PREPARATION TIME: 10 MINUTES • COOKING TIME: 5 MINUTES • ✓ DF

This is one of my favourites, a real Bangkok staple, and my ultimate comfort food whenever I find I'm missing Thailand. I like to serve it as a single meal over a plate of plain rice, with a Thai-style fried egg on top, just waiting to ooze out its yellow goodness. It provides a creamy counterbalance to the salty-spiciness of the dish.

4–6 **bird's-eye chillies**
1 **medium–large red chilli**,
    cut into chunks
6 cloves of **garlic**, peeled
a pinch of **salt**
2 tablespoons **dark soy sauce**
1 tablespoon **light soy sauce**
1 tablespoon **nam pla** (fish sauce)
a pinch of **granulated sugar**
1–2 tablespoons **vegetable oil**

200–300g **beef**, minced or
    finely chopped
100g **green beans**, topped, tailed
    and cut into 1cm pieces
a large handful of **picked
    bai krapow**, or **Thai holy
    basil leaves** – the more the
    merrier – plus a few to scatter
    at the end

1. In a pestle and mortar, pound the chillies, garlic and salt together into a rough paste, then set aside.

2. Now mix the soy sauces, nam pla and 2 tablespoons of water together in a small bowl, and stir in the sugar. (This is a short cut to speed things up at the wok. Properly, you should add them individually.)

3. Heat the oil in a wok until it's really hot. Throw in the chilli-garlic paste and stir-fry for a few seconds – until you can really smell everything in the pan, but not long enough to colour the garlic. Add the beef and stir-fry until it's almost cooked through. Then add the green beans and keep stir-frying until the beef is done.

4. Finally, add the soy sauce mixture and stir, keeping it moving in the wok and allowing it to bubble up before adding the basil and wilting it into the dish.

5. Serve over steamed Thai jasmine rice, and finish with a scattering of a few extra basil leaves.

6. For a very Thai touch, heat about a 2–3cm depth of vegetable oil in another wok and, when it's super-hot, crack in an egg. Fry until the white is crispy on the outside, and the yolk runny within – it should take about a minute. Drain, and serve on top of your pad krapow and rice. Everyone should have their own egg, or there'll be fighting.

TIPS

* You can really use anything you like in this: prawns, duck, tofu, chicken, finely sliced beef, and so on.

* If you can't find Thai holy basil, you can substitute it with *bai horapha* (sweet basil), or regular basil.

* Traditionally, this is served with some nam pla prik on the side. To make this, chop up a few bird's-eye chillies and cover with 2–3 tablespoons of nam pla.

REALLY FAST
DESSERTS

Banana & Flake Ice Cream Surprise

SERVES 8 • PREPARATION TIME: 5 MINUTES PLUS FREEZING • COOKING TIME: NONE • V

Katie says: 'Like so many of us, I'm keen to please and yet have precious little time for faffing around. This dessert, which comes from an idea from my friend Julia Parker, falls into the winning category of being (a) popular with all ages, (b) phenomenally straightforward and cheap, and yet (c) looks really rather snazzy.'

> a tub of inexpensive **vanilla ice cream**
> 2 **bananas**, peeled
> 2 **chocolate flakes**

1. Empty the tub of ice cream into a bowl that you can put into the freezer. Let it warm up just a little so that you can work with it and mix it around a bit. Mash the bananas and stir them into the ice cream. Smooth it all over.

2. Bash up the chocolate flakes and sprinkle them generously on top. Put in the freezer until you're ready to serve. (We told you it was easy.)

TIPS

* We've yet to meet a kid (or adult, for that matter) who doesn't love this. We're sure you can think of a whole host of additional surprises to mix into the ice cream (crumbled biscuits, perhaps? Raspberries?). Katie tends to hand the whole affair over to the kids who are going to eat it, and lets them get on with it.

Affogato Arabesque

SERVES 4 • PREPARATION TIME: 10 MINUTES • COOKING TIME: NONE • ♥ WF GF V

A Lebanese twist on an Italian classic.

1. Make your fresh coffee in your usual way, adding 2 cracked-open cardamom pods and their seeds to the grounds (we find one of those Italian, hob-top espresso pots the best for this).

2. Place a scoop of a good vanilla ice cream into each of 4 bowls. Serve with a shot of espresso on the side. Then pour the espresso over the ice cream, and enjoy!

Henry's Salted Caramel Bananas

SERVES 4 • PREPARATION TIME: 1 MINUTE • COOKING TIME: 15 MINUTES • WF GF V

4 **bananas**, peeled
25g **butter**
100g **caster sugar**
a good pinch of **sea salt**
25ml **brandy** (optional)

1. Slice the bananas in half lengthways. Heat the butter in a pan and fry the bananas until they're a little brown.

2. Sprinkle on the caster sugar and the sea salt, and cook until the caster sugar has caramelized. Then, if you like, flame it with the brandy (not necessary, but fun).

3. Serve with vanilla ice cream.

Lychees with Fresh Ginger & Sherry

SERVES 2–4 • PREPARATION TIME: 10 MINUTES • COOKING TIME: 5 MINUTES • WF GF DF V

Sweet, honey-ish lychees, spiky fresh ginger and mellow sherry.

1 x 567g tin of **lychees**, drained save for 12 tablespoons of liquid
100ml **medium sherry**
a 1cm piece of **fresh ginger**, peeled and finely julienned
4 **ice cubes**, crushed

1. Put the drained lychees into a small bowl, cover and refrigerate until needed. Pour the reserved lychee liquid, sherry and the ginger into a small pan. Bring to the boil, then turn down the heat and simmer for a few minutes, or until slightly reduced and thickened. Remove from the heat and leave to cool. When completely cold, cover and place in the fridge to chill.

2. Divide the chilled lychees between 4 glasses. Pop a spoonful of crushed ice into each glass and stir quickly. Pour over the sherry/ginger mixture. Stir again. Serve.

Prosecco & Nectarines

SERVES 4 • PREPARATION TIME: 5–10 MINUTES • COOKING TIME: NONE • WF GF DF V

This dessert is super-quick and super-simple – sort of a deconstructed Bellini.

4 ripe **nectarines**, peeled, stoned and cut into cubes
juice of ½ a **lemon**
1–2 tablespoons **icing sugar** (or to taste)
250ml **prosecco**
raspberries, to serve (optional)

1. Put the nectarines, lemon juice and sugar into a clean bowl, toss together and leave to stand for 5 minutes.

2. Then divide them between 4 coupes and pour prosecco over each one. Top with fresh raspberries if you like. Make sure the fruit is at room temperature and that the wine is nice and cold.

CONVERSION CHART FOR COMMON MEASURES

LIQUIDS

15 ml	½ fl oz
25 ml	1 fl oz
50 ml	2 fl oz
75 ml	3 fl oz
100 ml	3½ fl oz
125 ml	4 fl oz
150 ml	¼ pint
175 ml	6 fl oz
200 ml	7 fl oz
250 ml	8 fl oz
275 ml	9 fl oz
300 ml	½ pint
325 ml	11 fl oz
350 ml	12 fl oz
375 ml	13 fl oz
400 ml	14 fl oz
450 ml	¾ pint
475 ml	16 fl oz
500 ml	17 fl oz
575 ml	18 fl oz
600 ml	1 pint
750 ml	1¼ pints
900 ml	1½ pints
1 litre	1¾ pints
1.2 litres	2 pints
1.5 litres	2½ pints
1.8 litres	3 pints
2 litres	3½ pints
2.5 litres	4 pints
3.6 litres	6 pints

WEIGHTS

5 g	¼ oz
15 g	½ oz
20 g	¾ oz
25 g	1 oz
50 g	2 oz
75 g	3 oz
125 g	4 oz
150 g	5 oz
175 g	6 oz
200 g	7 oz
250 g	8 oz
275 g	9 oz
300 g	10 oz
325 g	11 oz
375 g	12 oz
400 g	13 oz
425 g	14 oz
475 g	15 oz
500 g	1 lb
625 g	1¼ lb
750 g	1½ lb
875 g	1¾ lb
1 kg	2 lb
1.25 kg	2½ lb
1.5 kg	3 lb
1.75 kg	3½ lb
2 kg	4 lb

OVEN TEMPERATURES

110°C......(225°F).......Gas Mark ¼
120°C......(250°F).......Gas Mark ½
140°C......(275°F).......Gas Mark 1
150°C......(300°F).......Gas Mark 2
160°C......(325°F).......Gas Mark 3
180°C......(350°F).......Gas Mark 4
190°C......(375°F).......Gas Mark 5
200°C......(400°F).......Gas Mark 6
220°C......(425°F).......Gas Mark 7
230°C......(450°F).......Gas Mark 8

MEASUREMENTS

5 mm .... ¼ inch
1 cm .... ½ inch
1.5 cm .... ¾ inch
2.5 cm .... 1 inch
5 cm .... 2 inches
7 cm .... 3 inches
10 cm .... 4 inches
12 cm .... 5 inches
15 cm .... 6 inches
18 cm .... 7 inches
20 cm .... 8 inches
23 cm .... 9 inches
25 cm .... 10 inches
28 cm .... 11 inches
30 cm .... 12 inches
33 cm .... 13 inches

Working with different types of oven

All the recipes in this book have been tested in an oven without a fan. If you are using a fan-assisted oven, lower the temperature given in the recipe by 20°C. Modern fan-assisted ovens are very efficient at circulating heat evenly around the oven, so there's also no need to worry about positioning.

Regardless of what type of oven you use you will find that it has its idiosyncrasies, so don't stick slavishly to any baking recipes. Make sure you understand how your oven behaves and adjust accordingly.

Key to Symbols/Nutritional Info

♥   LOW SATURATED FATS
✓   LOW GLYCAEMIC (GI) LOAD
WF   WHEAT FREE
GF   GLUTEN FREE
DF   DAIRY FREE
V   VEGETARIAN
🐦   COOKING TIPS, EXTRA INFORMATION
TIPS   AND ALTERNATIVE IDEAS.

Index

An Hachette UK Company
www.hachette.co.uk

First published in Great Britain in 2014
by Conran Octopus Limited, a part of
Octopus Publishing Group, Endeavour House,
189 Shaftesbury Avenue, London WC2H 8JY
www.octopusbooks.co.uk

This book includes a selection of previously
published recipes taken from the following titles:
Leon Naturally Fast Food and *Leon Family & Friends*.

A CIP catalogue record for this book is
available from the British Library.

Publisher: Alison Starling
Senior Editor: Sybella Stephens
Assistant Editor: Meri Pentikäinen
Art Director: Jonathan Christie
Art Direction, Design and Illustrations:
    Anita Mangan
Additional illustrations: Ella MacLean
Design Assistant: Abigail Read
Photography: Georgia Glynn Smith
Production Manager: Katherine Hockley

ISBN 978 1 84091 671 3

Printed and bound in China

10 9 8 7 6 5 4 3 2

A note from the authors…
Medium eggs should be used unless
otherwise stated.
We have endeavoured to be as accurate as
possible in all the preparation and cooking
times listing in the recipes in this book.
However they are an estimate based on our
own timings during recipe testing, and should be
taken as a guide only, not as the literal truth.
We have also tried to source all our food facts
carefully, but we are not scientists. So our food
facts and nutrition advice are not absolute.
If you feel you require consultation with a
nutritionist, consult your GP for
a recommendation.

Also available in the Little Leon series...

*Breakfast & Brunch • Smoothies, Juices & Cocktails
Soups, Salads & Snacks • Brownies, Bars & Muffins • One Pot*